MAGNETS

Magic Forces

by Jim Pipe

Aladdin/Watts
London • Sydney

MAGNETS

You use **magnets** every day. Fridge **magnets** are used to stick pieces of paper to the door of a refrigerator.

Magnetic discs store information in computers. A magnetic video tape records sounds and pictures.

Fridge magnets

Computer

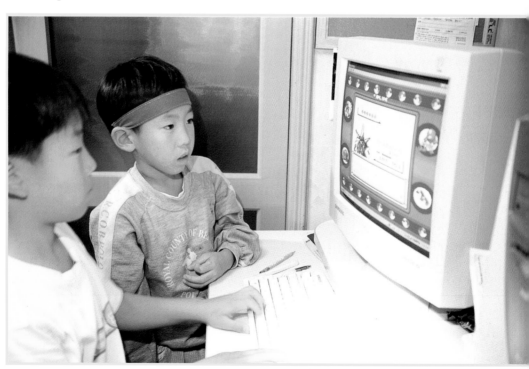

Many electrical machines use **magnets**.
There are **magnets** inside televisions and
telephones. **Magnets** are all around us!

Train
Powerful magnets
push this train along
a track.

Speakers
The speakers in a hi-fi
system use magnets to
make sounds louder.

Compass
The needle in a
compass is a magnet.
It always points north.

Nature's magnets
Dolphins and pigeons
have tiny magnets
inside their bodies.

FORCES

Pushes and pulls make things move.

We can pull a heavy log by pulling on a rope. A digger digs a hole by pushing and pulling earth.

Pushes and pulls are **forces**. We can see and feel how these **forces** make objects move.

Pulling

Pushing

However, some **forces** are invisible. We can't see what is pushing or pulling an object.

Magnets

Magnets create invisible **forces** that push these rings up the pole.

It's not magic, but the science of magnets!

Magnets are not the only invisible forces.

We can't see electricity, but it drives the motor in this tram and makes its lights shine.

What other forces can't you see? When you throw a ball into the air, something always pulls it down to the ground.

MAGNETS ATTRACT

Magnets can be different shapes and sizes. Some magnets are shaped like a bar.

A horseshoe magnet is a bar magnet bent into a 'U' shape. Magnets can also be shaped like marbles or round discs.

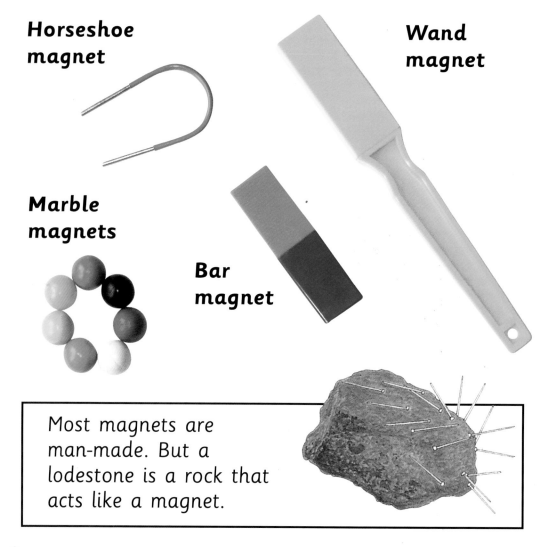

Horseshoe magnet

Wand magnet

Marble magnets

Bar magnet

Most magnets are man-made. But a lodestone is a rock that acts like a magnet.

If you bring a magnet near to a metal spoon, it pulls the spoon towards it. We say the magnet **attracts** the spoon.

This pull is called a magnetic force. To take the spoon away from the magnet, you have to pull them apart.

Magnet attracts a spoon

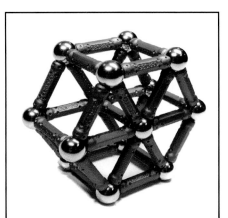

This model is made from magnets that attract each other.

The magnetic pieces in this game stick to the board.

Why do you think this makes it a good travel game?

MAGNETIC AND NON-MAGNETIC

Magnets only attract some materials. These are called **magnetic** materials.

Some screwdrivers are magnets. They can pick up steel screws and iron nails. Iron and steel are both **magnetic** materials.

Magnetic steel screws

In this doorbell, a magnet attracts an iron hammer.

The hammer hits a bell, which makes it ring!

Non-magnetic materials

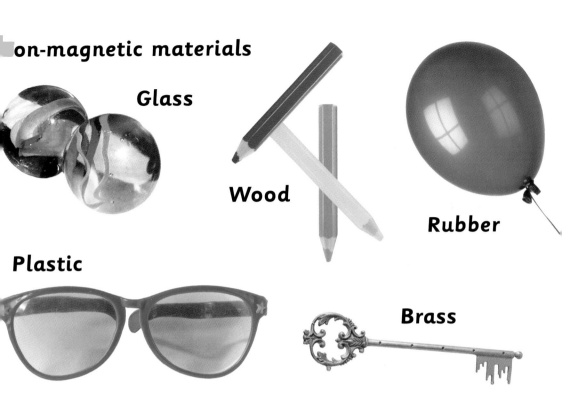

Glass

Wood

Rubber

Plastic

Brass

A magnet does not attract all metals.
It does not attract brass, copper or aluminium.

Magnets will not attract wood, plastic or glass
either. These are all **non-magnetic** materials.

Collect some different
objects and use a magnet
to see which are magnetic.

Make a list and put them
into two groups, magnetic
and non-magnetic.

POLES REPEL

The Earth itself is a giant magnet, and so are the Sun, other stars and most of the planets.

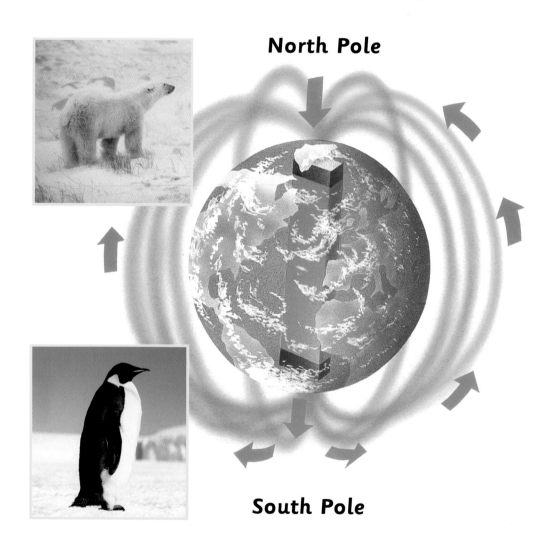

North Pole

South Pole

The Earth has two **poles**, a North and a South **Pole**. Penguins live near the South **Pole**. Polar bears live near the North **Pole**.

All magnets have two **poles**. On a bar magnet, the red end is the north **pole**. The blue end is the south **pole**.

A south **pole** and a north **pole** pull together, or attract each other.

Attract

Repel

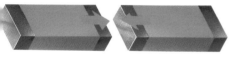

When two north **poles** are put together, they push against each other. We say they **repel** each other.

This girl can't see the magnetic forces, but she can feel them pushing.

What do you think happens when two south poles are put together?

STRONG AND WEAK

Some magnets are very **strong**.

Maglev train

This is a Maglev train.
The train does not have an engine.
It is pushed along by magnets on a track.
It travels as fast as a plane!

This girl is using a big magnet to pick up paper-clips.

Do you think a weaker magnet will pick up more or fewer paper-clips? Is a smaller magnet always weaker?

This boy is testing his magnets to see which is **strongest**.

He puts a paper-clip at the top of a ruler.

He slowly moves the magnet closer to the paper-clip.

Testing magnets

Most fridge magnets are weak. They can pin a piece of paper to a fridge, but not heavy objects.

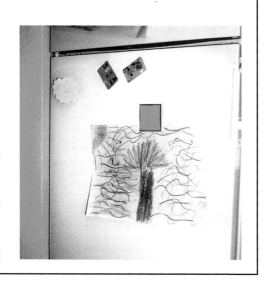

He sees where the paper-clip is pulled to the magnet.
He writes down the measurement.

A **strong** magnet pulls the paper-clip from far away. A **weak** magnet will need to be close to the paper-clip.

15

THROUGH PAPER AND GLASS

Magnetic forces can push and pull **through** materials.

A magnet can attract a paper-clip through a piece of **paper** or other non-magnetic materials such as wood and plastic.

Through paper

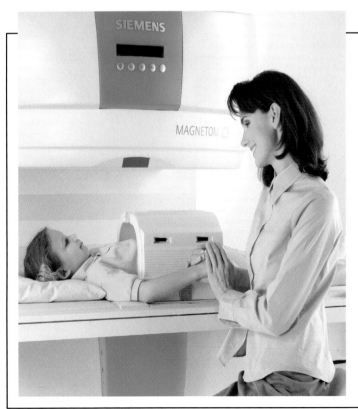

When electricity goes through you it can hurt.

When magnetic forces go through you it does not hurt. Magnets can help doctors to look inside us

Through a body

Through water

A magnet works **through** water. It can pull a paper-clip out of a jar filled with water.

Two magnets can attract each other **through** the **glass** on a fish tank.

When we move the outside magnet, the magnet on the inside rubs the **glass** clean!

Through glass

Glass

Why do you think that magnets are used to clean the inside of a fish tank?

COMPASS

A **compass** helps people to find their way. Walkers, sailors and pilots all use **compasses**.

The needle in a **compass** is a magnet. It always points north. The Earth is a giant magnet that attracts the **compass** needle.

Compas

Using a map and compass

This boy is making a **compass** with a bar magnet. He ties string around the middle of the magnet.

When the magnet stops spinning, its south pole points north. It is attracted by the Earth's North Pole.

Place a bar magnet close to a compass.

What do you think happens to the compass needle?

Bees, dolphins and lobsters have tiny magnets in their bodies.

The magnets help these animals to find their way on long journeys.

ELECTROMAGNETS

Some magnets are made by electricity. They are called **electromagnets**. Strong **electromagnets** can lift heavy loads of iron and steel.

When the electricity is switched off, an **electromagnet** lets go of its load.

Electromagnet

Permanent magnets

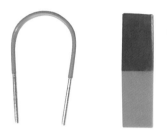

You can switch off an electromagnet.

But you can't switch off a bar or horseshoe magnet. These are called permanent magnets.

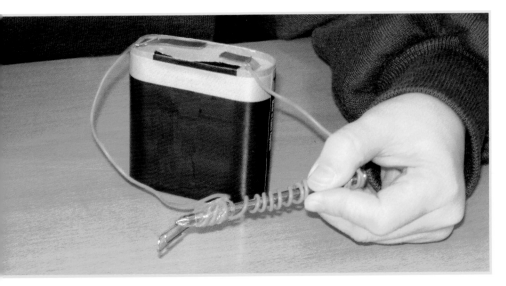

A simple electromagnet

Here is a simple **electromagnet**.
Some plastic-covered wire is wrapped
around a large nail.

The ends of the wire are attached to a battery.
The electricity flowing around the nail turns
the nail into an **electromagnet**.

Why are electromagnets
used for recycling rubbish?

Think about which materials
a magnet picks up, and
which ones it leaves behind.

Recycling

MOTORS, SPEAKERS AND DISCS

Headphones

Many electrical machines use electromagnets.

All electric **motors** contain magnets, from the engine in a car to the fan in a hair-dryer.

Any machine with a **speaker** has a magnet, such as a TV, telephone or headphones.

Car

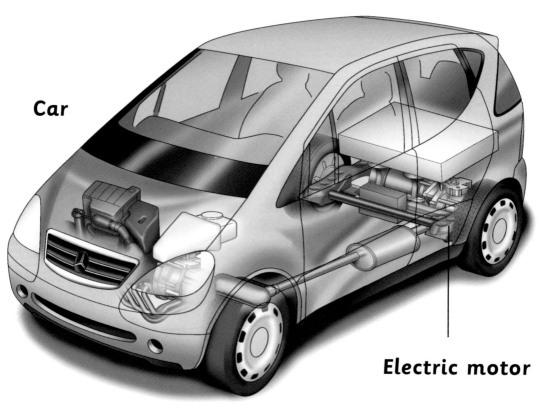

Electric motor

Magnetic discs

Magnets can also damage video and audio tapes and TVs. So be careful!

Computers use magnetic **discs** to store information.

You must not put a magnet on or near **discs** or computers as it can damage them.

Washing machines, electric drills and food mixers all have magnets in their motors.

Take a look around your house – what other machines with magnets can you find?

Electric drill

MAGNET MAGIC!

Look out for words and ideas about magnets.

It was Science Week at school. Billy's teacher put the class into groups. She asked each group to do a science project.

Tina Watts leaned over to Billy and said, "I bet our idea is better than yours." "Just you wait and see," said Billy.

Billy's group sat and thought... and thought. "What about building a space rocket?" said Pat. "Much too hard!" said Dave.

The next day, Billy
was walking past
Mrs Thomson's class.
He saw his friend Charlie
using a magnet to pick up
some paper-clips.

"That's it!" thought Billy.
He rushed back to tell the
rest of the group his idea.
"Magnets!" shouted Billy.

Tina was listening.
"Great idea, Billy," she said.
"We might use it too!"

Billy was furious.
"We'll just have to
make our project better,"
said Hannah.
"Let's meet up after school
to work something out."

The group met at Pat's house.
Hannah had borrowed a magnet kit from school.

Billy pushed a ring
magnet up a stick by
repelling it with
other ring magnets.

Dave picked up a chain of magnet marbles
using two wand magnets.

"What if we hide one of the magnets?" asked Billy. "Then no one can see what makes the project work," said Hannah.

"Great idea!" said Billy. "It can be a magnet magic show." "I'll hide a magnet in this wand to perform our tricks," said Dave.

Later that week it was the Science Fair. Each group took it in turn to show their project. Tina's group began their project with a fishing game.

"A magnet on the end of a line attracts the metal paper-clip on each fish," said Tina.

The second part was a
Treasure Island.
"You have to find the
treasure in the sand,"
explained Tina.

"The magnet attracts a
steel nut we put inside
the treasure box.
It won't pick up the sand
because it's non-magnetic."

It was time for Billy's
group to go.

"Abracadabra!"
shouted Billy.
"With my magic
wand I can make a
compass spin around."

28

Billy pointed the wand at the compass and the
needle spun around. Everyone clapped.

Hannah did the next trick.
Using the magic wand, she made a toy car
move across the table without touching it.

"Very good tricks!" said the teacher.
"How do they work?"

"We put a strong magnet at the end of the wand," said Dave. "It makes the compass needle spin around."

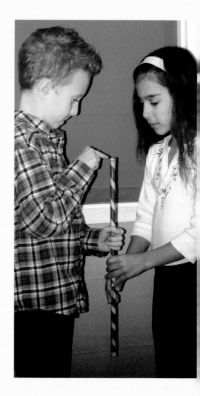

"The car also has a magnet on the back," said Hannah. "It repels the magnet on the wand, so the car moves!"

The teacher gave Billy and his friends first prize. Even Tina agreed that the magnetic wand was a great idea.

WRITE YOUR OWN STORY about using magnets. Or make a list of the things you can do with magnets. Then challenge a friend to do something from your list.

Can you?	Helpful Hints
Find magnetic materials	Mix iron nails and steel paper-clips up with non-magnetic objects.
Make magnets repel	Make sure similar poles are facing.
Attract through wood	Make sure the wood isn't too thick!
Attract through water	Drop a paper-clip into a glass of water.
Find hidden magnets in a room?	A compass can help – its needle moves when a magnet is near.

QUIZ

What are the two poles of a magnet called?

Answers on page 13

Can you think of three non-magnetic materials?

Answer on page 11

Why should you keep magnets away from computer discs?

Answer on page 23

How do these use magnets?

Doorbell   Bee

Compass

Speaker

Answers on pages 5, 10, 18, 19

INDEX

Note to Parents and Teachers

The READING ABOUT: STARTERS series introduces key science vocabulary and concepts to young children while encouraging them to discover and understand the world around them. The series works as a set of graded readers in three levels.

LEVEL 3: READ ALONE follows guidelines set out in the National Curriculum for Year 3 in schools. These books can be read alone or as part of guided or group reading. Each book has three sections:

• Information pages that introduce key concepts. Key words appear in bold for easy recognition on pages where the related science concepts are explained.
• A lively story that recalls this vocabulary and encourages children to use these words when they talk and write.
• A quiz asks children to look back and recall what they have read.

MAGIC FORCES looks at MAGNETS. Below are some answers and activities related to the questions on the information spreads that parents, carers and teachers can use to discuss and develop further ideas and concepts:

p. 7 *What other forces can't you see?* You could explain that when you throw a ball up into the air, gravity pulls it down to the ground. On a windy day, ask children to feel the wind pushing against them. They can feel its force, even if they can't see it.

p. 9 *Why do you think magnetic pieces make it a good travel game?* Because magnetic pieces stick to the board, they won't be spilled by the movement of a car or train.

p. 13 *What do you think happens when two south poles are put together?* Two south poles push against, or repel, each other, just like two north poles.

p. 14 *Do you think a weaker magnet will pick up more or less paper-clips? Will it be smaller?* The stronger a magnet is, the more paper-clips it will pick up. However, a big magnet is not necessarily stronger than a small one.

p. 17 *Why do you think that magnets are used to clean the inside of a fish tank?* Because the magnet outside the tank moves the magnet that is inside, there is no need to put your hand in the fish tank. This stops you from spreading germs that might harm the fish.

p. 19 *What do you think happens to a compass needle when you place a bar magnet close to it?* When it is close to the compass, the magnetic force of a bar magnet is stronger than the Earth's magnetic force, so it makes the compass needle turn towards it.

p. 21 *Why are electromagnets used for recycling rubbish?* Electromagnets are used to separate iron and steel from non-magnetic materials such as plastic and cardboard.

ADVISORY TEAM

Educational Consultant
Andrea Bright – Science Co-ordinator, Trafalgar Junior School, Twickenham

Literacy Consultant
Jackie Holderness – former Senior Lecturer in Primary Education, Westminster Institute, Oxford Brookes University

Series Consultants
Anne Fussell – Early Years Teacher and University Tutor, Westminster Institute, Oxford Brookes University

David Fussell – C.Chem., FRSC

CONTENTS

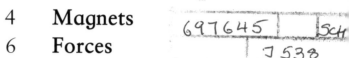

Billy and his friends use magnets
to amaze their classmates.

© **Aladdin Books Ltd 2005**

Designed and produced by
Aladdin Books Ltd
2/3 Fitzroy Mews
London W1T 6DF

First published in
Great Britain in 2005 by
Franklin Watts
96 Leonard Street
London EC2A 4XD

A catalogue record for this
book is available from the
British Library.

ISBN 0 7496 6252 2 (H'bk)

ISBN 0 7496 6387 1 (P'bk)

All rights reserved
Printed in Malaysia

Editor: Sally Hewitt
Design: Flick, Book Design
and Graphics
Thanks to:
• The pupils of Trafalgar Junior
School, Twickenham and St.
Paul's C.E. Primary School,
Addlestone, for appearing as
models in this book.
• Andrea Bright, Janice Bibby and
Stephanie Cox for helping to
organise the photoshoots.
• The pupils and teachers of
Trafalgar Junior School,
Twickenham and St. Nicholas
C.E. Infant School, Wallingford,
for testing the sample books.

Photocredits:
*l-left, r-right, b-bottom, t-top,
c-centre, m-middle*
Cover tl, tr & b, 2tl, 3, 5tl, 8 & 9
all, 11br, 13 both, 14br, 15tr, 16tr,
17tl, 19tr & br, 20tr, 21t, 22tr,
24bl, 25 both, 26-30 all, 31tr & ml
— Marc Arundale /Select Pictures.
Cover tm, 5tl, 14t — Shanghai
Maglev Transportation
Development Co. 2ml, 5mr, 12
both — Corbis. 2bl, 19mr, 31bcr —
Otto Rogge Photography. 4t, 5tl, 10
all, 15bl, 17mr & bl, 21br, 31bcl &
br — Jim Pipe. 4b — TongRo. 5bl,
11t all, 18 both, 23tl, 31mr, 31bl
— Ingram Publishing. 5br —
Digital Vision. 6tr — Brand X
Pictures. 6b — John Deere. 5br —
DAJ. 16bl — Siemens. 20b, 24mr
— Photodisc. 23tr — PBD. 23br —
cambridgeconsultants.com.